By Air, Sea, and Land

Diggers

Paul Strickland

WATERBIRD BOOKS
Columbus, Ohio

Bulldozer

Bulldozers are used to level the ground.

Dump Truck

Dump trucks take away rocks and dirt from construction sites.

More About Bulldozers

Instead of tires, bulldozers have tracks. Tracks are far stronger than wheels or tires. The metal treads dig into the ground. Then, the bulldozer can push dirt and rocks away.

More About Dump Trucks

A dump truck as large as this one can carry 50 tons of rock. The back of the dump truck can lift up at the front and dump its load out.

Tractor

This construction **tractor** can be used like a bulldozer or a digger.

More About Tractors

This construction tractor has a large bucket at the front that can scoop up large piles of soil. The bucket can also be used like a bulldozer to level the ground.

There is a backhoe at the back of the tractor. The backhoe can dig deep into the ground. This backhoe has a narrow bucket. It can be taken off and replaced with a backhoe that is a different size or shape.

Excavator

Excavators dig large holes before construction begins.

More About Excavators

Excavators dig holes like backhoes. Unlike a backhoe, it can rotate. It can dig dirt out of one place, spin around, and dump it somewhere else.

The teeth of the bucket are made of very hard metal.
Excavators are often used for digging out basements.
They dig the hole where the basement of a new house
will be.

Front-End Loader

Front-end loaders scoop up dirt and rocks.

More About Front-End Loaders

Front-end loaders come in all sizes. This one is mid-sized. It could fill a big pickup truck with one scoop. Using a loader is the quickest way to scoop dirt and rocks into a truck.

Front-end loaders are used for all kinds of different jobs.
They can carry out dirt and rocks at a construction site.
They can level the ground so that it is flat. They can also
carry large plants that are too heavy for people to carry.

Low-Loading Trailer

Low-loading trailers are used often to transport large construction vehicles.

More About Low-Loading Trailers

Low-loading trailers deliver large construction vehicles to
the construction site. They can travel quicker than
bulldozers and other construction vehicles. At the site,
the trailer lowers its ramp, and the bulldozer drives off.

Low-loading trailers also deliver other heavy objects, like large trees and piles of lumber. Sometimes, low-loading trailers even transport houses.

What Did You Learn?

Why is this loader and dumpster smaller than average?

How are these two machines different?

Why does this excavator have tracks?

How are these two machines different?

Small machines can often go where there is no room for big machines.

This excavator has tracks for moving over rocky or uneven ground.

This digger can lift and load.

This is a breaker. It is used for smashing concrete.

This bulldozer only pushes.

This digger is an old machine. It was built before hydraulic rams were invented. It is controlled by wire cables.

School Specialty
Children's Publishing

Copyright © Paul Stickland 1992, 2004
Designed by Douglas Martin.

This edition published in the United States of America in 2004 by
Waterbird Books,
an imprint of School Specialty Children's Publishing,
a member of the School Specialty Family.
8720 Orion Place, Columbus, OH 43240-2111
www.ChildrensSpecialty.com

Library of Congress Cataloging-in-Publication is on file with the publisher.

ISBN 0-7696-3374-9
Printed in China.
1 2 3 4 5 6 7 8 MP 08 07 06 05 04